THE NEED TO KNOW LIBRARY™

EVERYTHING YOU NEED TO KNOW ABOUT

TROLLS AND CYBERMOBS

SABRINA ADAMS

Rosen
YA™
New York

Published in 2018 by The Rosen Publishing Group, Inc.
29 East 21st Street, New York, NY 10010

Library of Congress Cataloging-in-Publication Data

Names: Adams, Sabrina, author.
Title: Everything you need to know about trolls and cybermobs / Sabrina Adams.
Description: New York : Rosen Publishing, 2018. | Series: The need to know library | Audience: Grades 7–12. | Includes bibliographical references and index.
Identifiers: LCCN 2017003231| ISBN 9781508174202 (library-bound) | ISBN 9781508174189 (pbk.) | ISBN 9781508174196 (6-pack)
Subjects: LCSH: Cyberbullying—Juvenile literature. | Online trolling—Juvenile literature. | Internet and teenagers—Juvenile literature.
Classification: LCC HV6773.15.C92 A33 2018 | DDC 302.34/302854678—dc23
LC record available at https://lccn.loc.gov/2017003231

Manufactured in China

CONTENTS

INTRODUCTION

We don't often think about it when we are posting on or visiting social media websites, but the internet can be a dangerous place. The online world has become a place where people behave differently than in the real world. In some cases, people become victims of harassment and bullying due to the unusually abusive nature of some internet users. These online realities have become such a problem that they spill over into the real world. Serious cases of cyberbullying and online harassment have cost people jobs, friendships, and, in some instances, even their lives.

In some cases, people have been pushed to dangerous limits as a result of being stalked online by cyberbullies. One instance includes a story from a September 19, 2014, article in *Newsweek* magazine about a woman who posted body-positive messages about herself. Bullies calling her stupid, fat, and ugly harassed her nonstop and even cost her the job she had at a nonprofit organization. Trolls who had never even met her posted false claims about her sexual misconduct. Then posts under her name with the heading "Do Not Hire" appeared, with claims that she would not make a good employee. This kept prospective employers from hiring her when they searched her name online. She committed suicide.

Protesters hold up signs of Rehtaeh Parsons to show their support for victims of cyberbullying and victimization on the internet.

Age does not seem to matter as far as cyber-bullying is concerned. According to *Newsweek,* a seventeen-year-old named Rehtaeh Parsons killed herself after being gang-raped at a party. Someone posted the photo of the rape on the internet, causing her extreme distress. A fourteen-year-old named Jamey Rodemeyer committed suicide after experiencing harassment online for being gay. One fourteen-year-old named Jill Naber killed herself after a photo of her top-less was viewed and shared to the point of becoming viral. Fatal incidences like these have only increased as the internet and social media become more and more a part of people's everyday lives.

The internet and social media now enter people's lives at an earlier age than ever. And the damage of internet trolling leaves a permanent footprint that the victim will not be able to shake for years to come. That's why it is important to try to understand where this type of behavior comes from, how it affects people, what people can do to avoid it, and how people can take care of themselves if they are ever a victim of online trolls or cybermobs.

CHAPTER ONE

TROLLS AND CYBERMOBS

O ver the past decade, the damage of trolls and cybermobs has increased, and it has had a profound impact on our youth. According to an article in *Time* magazine, 70 percent of 18- to 24-year-olds who use the internet have experienced some form of online harassment. Unfortunately, it comes in many forms.

WHAT IT IS

Two of the most damaging forms of online harassment are trolling and cybermobs. A troll is traditionally defined as a mythical creature, or goblin, hiding in caves or under bridges. In folklore, trolls often jump out at innocent passersby, harassing them and causing trouble. In a similar way, an online "troll" is someone who deliberately causes trouble online, posting insulting messages or trying to cause psychological damage to people. Their methods include threatening users on social media, publishing personal information, or humiliating people because of their race, sex, or body type. Trolling can be as simple as writing "You're an idiot" to as fiercely damaging as cursing at someone, putting down their efforts, or threatening them in some way. Only the more extreme examples offer cause for alarm and perhaps a more proactive reaction.

Some online trolls become part of a cybermob. That's a group of two or more people who gang up on someone to harass or terrorize that person online. The way a cybermob forms is that an online troll with many "friends" or "followers" requests that his or her followers post negative information on someone's social media account. The greater the number of people who follow the instructions, the larger the cybermob becomes, extending the reach of cybermobs quite far. Thus, cybermobs can be that much more damaging than the work of just one online troll.

CYBERMOBS: ALL KINDS OF TARGETS

Many preteens and teens are subject to online trolling and cybermobs, and even celebrities and the rich are subjected to cyberbullying. Shortly after the release of the 2016 version of the film *Ghostbusters*, in which Leslie Jones was a costar, people began posting racist, sexist, and overtly insensitive and insulting comments about her. She was harassed so badly on Twitter that she quit the social media site for a period of time.

The person who was caught trolling and encouraging the cybermob that harassed Jones was con-

Actress and comedian Leslie Jones (*pictured*) was harassed online by Milo Yiannopolis. The incident brought the issue of cyberbullying into the national conversation when the media began to report on it.

servative British journalist Milo Yiannopoulos. He was permanently banned from Twitter after it was found that he encouraged his 300 thousand followers to harass Jones.

Cybermobs cause damage to individuals for countless reasons, such as due to their weight, social standing, sexual orientation, or physical or mental disabilities.

However, not all targets of cybermobs are individuals. An organization can also be the target of a cybermob. This can be a group of angry individuals who want to show their distaste for a late video game launch or a product that does not work to their liking. Or they may want to attack some other act that has inadvertently displeased many people. For example, in 2011, a Manhattan dentist received a negative online review of her services. When the dentist asked the patient to remove the review because she thought it contained lies, the patient sued her. From that point on, people ganged up on the dentist's website, giving false reviews and saying terrible things about her. Their false claims included everything from saying she was sleeping with her patients to her having AIDS. She even started getting threatening phone calls at both her office and her home. Because she was being sued, her insurance rates were increased tremendously. Ultimately, she could no longer attract new patients or keep the old ones. Within a year, she was forced to close her dental practice.

Other organizations, such as schools, can be targeted. Hackers can attack a company's internet technology (IT) system and bring computer servers down. This can affect a school's grading systems or other data the school has on its students. It can also affect a company's financial security. Whether the target of the cybermob is an individual or an organization, the damage can be devastating.

Another type of engagement that emerges from online mobilization and may take the shape of harassment is a flash mob. A flash mob is a sudden and disruptive event in which a large group of people discover, via the internet, a plan to gather in the real world at a specific place and time. The crowd then gathers and suddenly appears in large numbers. The reasons for flash mobs can be to protest a law or event or simply to cause disruption. Police have a hard time handling flash mobs on such short notice. These gatherings demonstrate the impact and potential harm that a cybermob can have offline.

While some flash mobs may be destructive, some can be used to promote issues. This flash mob celebrates CDMX Mexico's pride at Palacio de Bellas Artes, a cultural center in Mexico City.

WHY DO PEOPLE HARASS?

What makes someone think it's alright to troll others, and what makes people follow them and join in? According to *Time* magazine, Milo Yiannopoulos, the journalist banned from Twitter for inciting a cybermob to harass actress Leslie Jones, explained his "defense," or mindset, about people who incite trolling and cybermobs. He said that trolling is a result of our increasingly politically correct society. He stated that trolling occurs because "human nature has a need for mischief… the space we're making for others to be bolder in their speech is some of the most important work being done today. The trolls are the only people telling the truth."

This type of thinking is certainly controversial, and it does not take into account the feelings of the victims of the cyberbullying. In fact, a 2014 study by the journal *Personality and Individual Differences* found a connection between people who identified themselves as internet trolls and people with the personality traits of selfishness and cruel behavior.

The internet is a relatively new invention in human history, so the social etiquette that people have taken so long to develop with face-to-face interactions doesn't apply online. Consequentially, people tend to say things online that they would not be inclined to say in person, in a face-to-face situation. Why does this happen? According to an article in the *Wall Street Journal,* a psychologist from the Massachusetts Institute of Technology claims that people do not have as much

IT'S NOT JUST ON SOCIAL MEDIA

Social media gets the most attention in terms of trolls and the damage they can do. However, trolling does not only happen on social media. Online video gaming is another place where trolls can take over a situation and make an experience difficult for an online user. Many video game consoles have the capability of going on-line, allowing users to play against each other in real time and talk to each other over headsets. This creates an anonymous social media component that fosters trolling and bullying behavior. Playing against strangers encourages that situation of anonymous comfort that can make trolls feel like they can harass other users with no consequences, similar to the way it happens in a so-cial media atmosphere. Players may gang up on each other or use distressing language to talk about each other, and in the virtual world, abuse can take a visually and perhaps even audi-bly sexualized form. The stress of online trolls in video games can be especially frustrating for young players. Rules put out by the gaming companies try to lessen or eliminate online trolls and their many forms of abuse, but the effects continue.

Online video games also have trolls and cybermobs. Similar precautions for dealing with them are necessary.

self-control on social media when they don't have to see the reaction of the person they are addressing.

On Facebook, for example, taking part in a post of a friend you know well may involve writing comments to people you have never met before. People realize they may never meet that person in real life or that person would never know who they were if they did meet them. The anonymous atmosphere puts people at ease to express their true opinions, poke fun at people they disagree with, and take part in controversial, insulting, or hurtful discussions.

TAKING IT TO THE EXTREME

There are extreme methods of harassment that reach into the real world, affecting the victim and his or her family members. This is severely harmful territory.

Take sexting as one example. Sexting is the practice of sending someone sexually explicit photos or messages over a mobile device. The practice itself is not meant to harass, but when someone ends a sexual relationship, the pictures may be used in a harassing way, much to the embarrassment of the person who sent the explicit photos. Some people who have become victims have had suggestive or overtly sexual photos used against them after they break up with their girlfriend, boyfriend, or spouse. In some cases, the photo may be posted online with the malicious intent of seeking revenge. The photo may then get many embarrassing or insulting comments, humiliating the person who had originally sent that image in the strictest confidence. And those comments can come not only from strangers, but also from personal acquaintances.

An activity similar to sharing sext messages is doxxing. Doxxing is publishing personal data online. The information can include anything from a person's home address or phone number to his or her social security number or the names and information of family members. This can be especially dangerous to people who have their social security numbers made available to the public. A stolen identity can ruin a person's credit for many years to come.

Another extreme activity is swatting, or calling emergency responders or SWAT teams to a person's house when it is not warranted. This is often done as a joke. Other times it is done maliciously. No matter the intention, swatting results in surprise and fear, and it can cause psychological and even physical harm to the victim.

This SWAT team is converging on a target. Sometimes, it is unclear whether a team's information is reliable.

THE CONSEQUENCES

There is a difference between the consequences of being bullied in person instead of online. Although bullying never has a positive effect, the effects of in-person bullying can end. At a school, for example, the bully can get into trouble and be forced to deal with the behavior in a constructive manner. The bully might even develop a friendlier demeanor.

But neither of these outcomes is guaranteed. What is more likely is that exposure to a bully is limited to a specific class or setting. And, changing schools may mean being completely removed from the bully's pres-

When employers check references for potential employees, they may also check the job candidate's presence on social media. Evidence of trolling or being trolled can ruin a candidate's chances.

ence. The incidences might have less of an effect over time, depending on how traumatic they are. And the footprint for those incidents, if it consists only of people's memories, may fade.

The online bully, however, can do permanent damage because our online footprints are difficult, if not impossible, to remove from the internet. A person's ability to attract an employer can be severely impaired if prospective employers always find distasteful and negative information about the candidate when searching his or her name. People who post embarrassing images of their ex-boyfriend or ex-girlfriend can damage that person's ability to be in another relationship, and it can cause differences in other interpersonal relationships in the offline world.

Regardless of the long-term implications, the historical impact of in-person bullying and cyberbullying on the victim is that they each leave behind the same types of trauma, including the type that causes a person to completely lose the ability to cope.

MYTHS AND FACTS

MYTH: Trolling is anonymous.

FACT: Some trolls do try to stay anonymous, and others don't. Some may even use false names when posting insults so they can hide their identities. However, authorities are able to work with internet providers to find the true identity of an online user.

MYTH: Victims cannot overcome the damage of trolling.

FACT: While many victims suffer deeply from the effects of online cyberbullying, trolling, and cybermobs, they can still recover from the damage with time, effort, and help from friends, family, or professionals. It can take time, but many people can recover from the effects of the victimization.

MYTH: All people who take part in trolling and cybermobs also act like bullies when offline.

FACT: While trolls and people who take part in cybermobs often show the same characteristics as in-person bullies, not all of them act this way in their everyday lives. Because online bullies feel like they can do their damage anonymously or think they will have no chance of being caught, they may be much meaner on the internet than when not online. This sense of false freedom and anonymity may be what makes the proportion of online bullies larger than it is in offline life, making the internet a particularly dangerous place for those who are vulnerable to being victimized.

CHAPTER TWO

HOW CAN YOU PROTECT YOURSELF AND OTHERS?

Avoiding being a victim of cybermobs and trolling isn't always possible, and victims are not to blame when the problem does arise. However, there are some measures that people can take to help prevent the problem. There are also things people can do to keep an eye out for friends who might fall victim to online abuse.

DON'T PARTICIPATE IN SEXTING

Sexting, even in apps such as Snapchat where photos are meant to disappear shortly after being delivered, can be a very risky move. While written messages provide a record of thoughts and ideas only, they can still be very personal. Photos provide a captured moment of space and time that offers even more context for forming a memory. Videos may be the most personal and memorable of all, providing an opportunity to relive a moment with both sound and moving pictures. Kik Messenger, WhatsApp, Instagram, and even Tumblr are popular sites for social networking. People in relationships often use them by sharing an account, and individuals continue on with these social networks in some form or other even after relationships have dissolved. No one in a relationship thinks that they will be betrayed at the time they are taking sexually explicit photos because they trust their girlfriend or boyfriend. But the consequences of sexting often lead people to regret that act later on. The consequences of sexting messages, photos, or videos can be severe.

The mobile app Snapchat was designed so that users could share short-lived messages that delete themselves. This made it a popular choice for people interested in sexting.

Young people, in particular, are vulnerable because sexting has become a widespread issue among teens. According to dosomething.org, nearly 40 percent of teens have posted or sent sexually suggestive messages over the internet or on social media sites in the form of written, photographed, or recorded content. In total, 61 percent of people who have sent nude pictures of themselves through sexting admit that they did it because they felt pressured to do it. In addition, 17 percent of sexters share the messages they received with other people. More than half of those people have shared it with more than one person. This can leave quite a bit of material for trolls and cybermobs to take advantage of.

As the statistics suggest, sexting can cause a once-trusting and private moment to become very public. Not everyone knows that their photos were shared, but the people who do know have an even more troubling problem. Some sexting photos go viral, and some end up on revenge porn websites. These are websites where people post photos of their exes so that other people can view and download them.

In September 2016, a 31-year-old Italian woman named Tiziana Cantone found herself in the middle of a sex-tape controversy. The video was leaked by her ex-boyfriend and went viral on the internet. Her shame and embarrassment became overwhelming when her friends and family became aware of the situation, and she committed suicide.

The only way to stop people from sharing your photos is to not give them away in the first place.

CHANGE THE SUBJECT

Suppose you find yourself getting into a heated conversation with someone online. It may take some restraint to keep the discussion under control. Keep in mind the importance of online etiquette, even if the other people you are chatting with are not keeping their cool. If you find that the people you are chatting with are saying things that would sound especially confrontational if they were said in person, then that's a great clue that you should back off, change the subject, or completely leave the conversation. There is nothing that someone says or does online that should make you stoop to the level of a troll.

Changing the subject can be a good way to focus the conversation on something more positive and less controversial or mean-spirited. If changing the subject does not work, get out of the conversation. Remember that anything you post is your choice, and no one can force you to continue posting, responding, and conversing. Using self-control can get you a long way in keeping a positive demeanor online.

If changing the subject and getting out of the conversation does not work, it's time to unfriend or block the people who are bothering you. A troll can get out of hand and turn into a cybermob. But if just half of a cybermob were blocked from being able to communicate with you on social media, then a problem might be able to shrink instead of grow further out of control. Blocking people can loosen a great strain on someone who is experiencing the problem.

It's important to remember that you have a choice in whether you engage in online conversations. It's best to walk away from confrontational interactions.

Staying off social media sites can also help with avoiding trolls. According to *Newsweek* magazine, the likelihood of someone being victimized online strongly correlates with, or is constant with, the amount of time the person spends online. In other words, someone who is online all the time will be that much more exposed to trolls and cybermobs than someone who isn't online very much.

LOOK OUT FOR FRIENDS

You may be a witness to abuse directed toward people you care about. Friends are a valuable part of life, and it hurts to see them become victims of bullying, trolling, or online cybermobs. Fortunately, there are steps available for protecting friends from online trolling.

Keeping a lookout for friends being mentioned online in a negative way is one way to help. It may feel like a natural response to get into an argument with someone who is bad-mouthing a friend, but think twice before stepping in. Acting like a troll, or even responding to a troll, is not a helpful way to defend a friend, and it could make matters worse. Not only would you be hurting people, but you can be held accountable for your actions, too, because people who are caught trolling can face a harassment lawsuit. Even when the troll is anonymous, the internet provider that hosted the trolling event can be called to court if the victim takes action to prosecute the abuse. This will put the burden to find the troll into the hands of the website or web server provider, causing it to go through its records to find the person involved. So any action to combat trolling should model upstanding manners, and any action that takes on the shape of trolling can be recorded and tracked down to the source.

Another action to combat trolling that attacks a friend is sharing what you know with your friend. Let that friend know because you would want your friend to do the same for you. Explain why you think your

It's hard to bring bad news to a friend, but letting the friend know what is happening will help with figuring out how to deal with the problem.

friend should be concerned about the posts if you think the posts do merit concern. Reassure the friend that it's obvious that the comments are unfair and untrue. Bringing the problem up to the friend can help create awareness for the problem and let him or her know that a support system exists.

"SIT WITH US" APP

Today's teens and preteens use the internet and technology so much that it can be hard to separate the social world online from the social world in real life. One teen from California, Natalie Hampton, remembers what it was like to suffer socially and to be the victim of bullying. In an interview with the *Los Angeles Daily News*, she revealed that she sat alone at lunch during her entire year of seventh grade. Knowing how cruel people can be, and also how much teens use technology, she developed a mobile app, Sit With Us. It helps students who might be victims of bullying to quietly and anonymously find someone to sit with at lunch. The app helps people reach out and find someone in their school who would like to reach out and make others feel welcome. It helps connect people privately and avoids public rejection. Students who sign up to invite others to join them are called "ambassadors," and they can set up an open lunch for others to join. When fighting bullying, it helps to take the opposite approach of a troll!

Social media can be used for good and for bad. A mobile app called Sit With Us helps teens find people willing to make new friends.

CONTROLLING COMMENTERS AND HACKERS

Trolls and cybermobs tend to leave deliberately offensive comments on blogs in addition to social media sites. Running a blog allows the option of reviewing comments made by readers before they are published on the site. It is also possible to ban a person who has caused trouble on the site in the past and to reprimand users who don't follow the rules or use common courtesy. If a blog gets out of control with negative comments and threats, then the person who runs the blog can remove the comments and even report particularly threatening comments to the police before deleting them. These are all important options to be aware of when setting up a website and administering it.

Remember that if a person is mean enough to post negative comments, then that person may have the potential to do even worse if given the chance. Some trolls can bring their intentionally hurtful behaviors to the next level by hacking and interfering with a person's personal information online. Users make a hacker's job much easier when they set the security of an account to low. When setting up social media accounts and blogs, be sure to make the account as private as possible. Do not post location information, home addresses, or information that identifies family or friends. Also, be sure to make passwords as secure as possible by including capital and lowercase letters, numbers, and

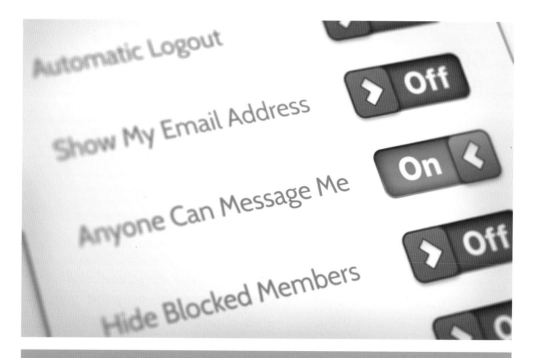

Adjusting social media settings can keep people from seeing personal information about you. It can also help you block trolls, cyberbullies, and other people you don't want to interact with.

symbols. It's also a good idea to make Instagram and other social media profiles private to thwart the work of trolls and hackers. A public profile means that anyone who simply looks up your name can have a window into your personal life, including all of your posts and information about where you might be (in written details or photos) or what you might be doing.

CHAPTER THREE

WHAT IF IT HAPPENS TO YOU?

S ometimes, despite our best efforts, we may become the victims of trolls or cybermobs. In such times, it is important to know how to minimize the difficulties that the problem causes.

First and foremost, realize that you are not the first person, nor will you be the last, to experience being targeted. Over 25 percent of teens say they have been cyberbullied repeatedly, according to studies by the i-SAFE foundation, an organization dedicated to internet safety. But just as others have suffered, there are many who have recovered.

DON'T FEED THE TROLLS

When faced with trolls who are harassing you or your friend, it might seem tempting to fight back and defend yourself or a friend. But this is usually exactly what trolls and cyberbullies are looking for. When you acknowledge a troll's hurtful comments, you have let him or her know that the efforts were successful and that you were affected. This often makes the troll feel in control of the situation and even more motivated to continue and escalate the abusive behavior.

If a troll meets nothing but silence, there is nothing for him or her to feed off of. There is no back-and-forth argument about anything. The person who is being trolled gains a certain power by not responding. After a while, the troll looks foolish by continuing to have a one-sided argument.

The same is true for cybermobs. After a while of people ganging up on the same person with no response, the fight begins to lose its steam. The crowd may naturally dissipate over time. But if the target of the cybermob responds, the whole crew has something to feed off of. The cycle may continue, and the abuses may even escalate. Responding certainly does not mean that the victim is to blame for the abuses, but keeping quiet can be an effective way to quell the anger of trolls and cybermobs.

Blocking a troll from your social media accounts is another good way to stop the damage from reaching into your world. Trolls know that when they make a comment on your page, all of your contacts, friends, and family members who are connected with you on social media will be able to read it. Because of this, even if it is your intention to ignore the troll, the troll may be able to attract the attention of the people who are close to you. Take immediate action to stop the person and block him or her from being able to insult you. Don't be afraid to block a lot of people, either. If a cybermob develops from an overabundance of trolls, block as

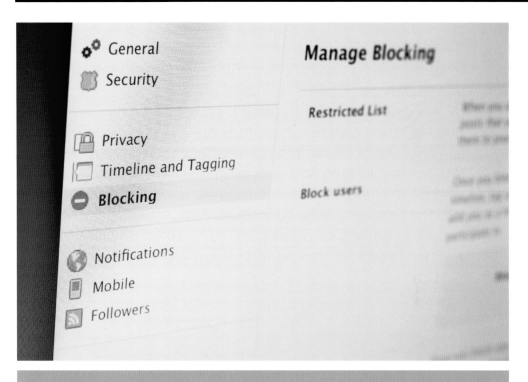

This is the page that shows Facebook's options for blocking users. Blocking those who have caused trouble is a good way to make social media safer and more enjoyable.

many as you can and then tell the administrators of the website about your problem. You may be able to report them on a large scale by allowing the administrators to locate a lot of them in one place.

DON'T GO IT ALONE

Getting help is an important tip for people who have been trolled or victimized by cybermobs. Telling a friend about the problem can be a good first step toward solving the problem. By telling someone, the victim can gain essential moral support.

According to i-SAFE, more than half of young people don't tell their parents when they are cyberbullied. This is a mistake because the consequences of cyberbullying can last longer, and can even reappear years later without warning, if a knowledgeable adult isn't brought into the picture. Some consequences of cyberbullying, including anxiety or depression, may last many years if a victim is unwilling to address them.

Imagine a vertical line down the middle of this photo. This offers a visual representation of how many teens hide from their parents that they have been victimized by cyberbullying.

In addition to telling a friend about a cyberbully or potential cyberbullying problem, it's important to also tell a trustworthy adult. If you don't feel that you can tell your parent, consider other trustworthy adults in your life. Even if the bullying behavior does not come from a student inside your school, telling a teacher or guidance counselor is another good option. These school professionals are trained to help students deal with problems and report issues to the appropriate authorities, potentially including the police. Ultimately, telling a teacher or other adult can mean the difference between continuing to be cyberbullied and getting the behavior to stop.

Adults can help teens and other young people report the bullying if they hadn't thought of doing it before. In some mild cases of trolling, a parent or other adult can get the behavior to stop by reporting it to schools or other parents if the culprit is a student who attends that school. Even the parents of a bully will likely want the bullying behavior to stop. Trolls and members of cybermobs often wish to retain their anonymity, so when they are found out, they

Seeking advice and counsel from mental health professionals or school guidance counselors can help victims heal from what happened.

may be inclined to stop their behavior. Being discovered may be a failure for them, and they will not likely want to face the consequences of failing to keep the activity hidden.

To deal with extreme or persistent cases, adults may help with pursuing legal options to get the bullying to stop. Adults should be involved in issues like having revenge porn removed from a website or pressing charges with the police to remedy the crime of cyberharassment or distribution of sexual material containing minors. If one adult doesn't respond in a way that seems normal or refuses to address the problem, feel free to bring the issue to another.

When someone attempts to inform a trusted party of a bad experience, it is important to mention the website where the problems began. That way, adults can easily figure out how to have website administrators ban, reprimand, or address the troll or cybermob at the site of the violation.

Users can even go directly to website administrators. Facebook, Instagram, and other sites allow users to report abuses. For Facebook, the link next to each post allows the user to review a dropdown menu of choices, which includes a choice called "Report." This link will allow the user to describe the problem with the post, message, or link that makes the user feel threatened. Similarly, Instagram has options to report abuses anonymously. Those websites don't share what users report with the person who posted the insulting or threatening comment.

And, they often agree to cooperate with the authorities because they care about fostering a safe space for their users.

No matter what you decide to do, it will help to make a printout or screen grab of bullying messages or encounters with trolls or cybermobs. Trolls may delete their comments if they feel as if they might be caught. If you have a hard copy of the encounter, you can show it as proof that it happened. It would be especially useful as evidence to bring to school officials or police officers. If the screen does not show it, add the date and time that the messages were received. This can help adults look into the issue further.

CALL THE POLICE

Cyberbullying is a crime, and it is harassment. Even the instructions for reporting abusive behavior on Facebook advise victims to contact the police if they are being threatened or if they fear for their safety. Many police departments have a cyberbullying division, which investigates cybercrimes such as the work of trolls and cybermobs. Even the Federal Bureau of Investigation (FBI) may oversee cybercrime divisions. Their activity may be to prevent widespread hacking of corporations or identity theft. However, local cybercrime units may also deal on a more local level with catching dangerous trolls. Threats are investigated and treated as harassment and public endangerment. Trolls that threaten vio-

Many police departments have divisions dedicated to cybercrimes. These crimes range from harassment to threats to extortion.

lence, rape, or death can and should meet harsh consequences for their actions.

To measure the severity of a cyber threat, authorities measure the intent of the person or people making the threat. For example, just as someone who has hit someone else with their car intentionally will get a harsher penalty than someone who does it accidentally, cyber-harassment is dealt with in a similar way. Someone who makes intentional, dangerous, and repeated threats to someone's safety will be considered to be a more dangerous threat than someone who uses bad language or insults someone without the threat of physical violence. While both types of threats may be punish-able depending on the circumstances, physical threats of violence are given the most serious punishment under the law.

Incidences of physical threat or violence require only one incident in order to be considered harassment under the law. Calling the police and getting them involved in incidences of trolling should happen right away. When reporting a crime to the police, you will be asked to provide as many details as possible about the attack or threat. You will have to give some personal information, such as your name, address, and other details. You may even be asked to testify, or tell the exact details of an incident, in a court of law if the cybercriminal is caught. If you and the website where the incident occurred provide enough proof of wrongdoing and malicious intent, the person accused of cyberbullying can be brought to justice.

New laws can give victims legal recourse to cut down on the damage done by sexting and revenge porn. A bill known as the Intimate Privacy Protection Act of 2016 may make it a crime to send and distribute sexually explicit photos or videos without the consent of the people involved—if it passes. Revenge porn laws are also cropping up in states around the United States. The laws vary from state to state. In Virginia, for example, revenge porn is a misdemeanor. It can earn the culprit a hefty fine of about $2,500, and up to a year in jail. In Illinois, revenge porn is a felony, which can mean imprisonment for more than a year and the loss of the right to vote during incarceration. More than 34 states have revenge porn laws, put in place under the Cyber Civil Rights Initiative. Some states consider the first offense as a misdemeanor and subsequent offenses as felonies. Other states consider the harshest threats of violence or death as felonies, while lesser threats are considered misdemeanors.

THEY REALLY DO GET CAUGHT

Many cyber trolls get what they have coming to them—by getting caught and being put in jail. One internet troll named Sean Duffy began harassing people on Facebook in 2010. The 25-year-old began trolling the tribute page of a 16-year-old girl who died in a car accident. He crossed out the eyes on her photos and drew stitches on her mouth to mock her death. Under one of the pictures, he wrote, "used car for sale, one useless owner."

Shortly after, Duffy began harassing the tribute pages of other teenage girls who died. He was caught when he began creating his own fake tribute pages and Facebook groups to mock real teens who had died. In one case, the page was a fake tribute to a teen, Natasha MacBryde, who had killed herself by throwing herself in front of a train. Duffy labeled the page Tasha the Tank Engine and superimposed her face onto a photo of the fictional character Thomas the Tank Engine. In another case, Duffy created a group to "honor" a girl who had been stabbed to death. He used a bloody knife as the profile picture and made a video that featured slashes on the girl's face.

When Duffy crossed the line from commenting on existing pages to creating his own, he was able to be caught more easily by authorities. When someone creates a page, the website can locate the person more easily than when anonymous posts are made on other sites. In 2011, Duffy received a sentence of 18 weeks in jail. He was also banned from using social network sites for a period of five years.

While it becomes easier for police to identify a troll with each offense, it only takes one offense to get them on the trail of an offender. Facebook and other social media sites routinely cooperate with the police to investigate criminal matters. They might give the information of a user under investigation. This can lead police to the real identity of an anonymous or fraudulent user.

10 GREAT QUESTIONS TO ASK A POLICE OFFICER ABOUT TROLLS AND CYBERMOBS

1. How are the cyberbullying laws in my state different from those in other states?
2. If I cyberbully a classmate, is the school responsible for my punishment or will I be reported to the police?
3. If I am cyberbullied, trolled, or the victim of a cybermob, should my family get me an attorney?
4. If my state does not have specific laws against cyberbullying, does that mean I will not get in trouble for doing it in school?
5. How do I report a troll?
6. How do police find trolls and members of cybermobs?
7. What should I do if I am wrongly accused of trolling or being in a cybermob?
8. Is trolling more dangerous than real-life bullying?
9. How often are trolls and members of cybermobs caught?
10. Where can my family get help if we need to protect ourselves from trolls online?

CHAPTER FOUR

HEALING FROM CYBER ATTACKS

O nce the damage by a troll or cybermob is done, it can take a long time to heal. What might have taken a short time to do on the internet can take a long time to undo in real life. In the most serious and tragic cases, the healing never happens. However, this does not have to happen if the victim immediately reaches out for support to the right groups to overcome the damage that has been suffered.

TRUSTING PEOPLE YOU KNOW

Choosing the right support system is important for overcoming the stress of being targeted. A close friend, parent, or adult can provide support like no one else can. Just knowing that someone else understands what the victim is going through and knows what the victim is trying to do can be a great help psychologically. Someone that the victim is close to can help check on the victim's progress or make sure the he or she is doing well emotionally. The victim should be sure to let this close friend or trustworthy adult know how he or she feels, instead of carrying all of those emotions on his or her own.

Getting help from a trusted adult is necessary because this person may be able to direct the victim to the type of support that can be helpful. The victim might benefit from group or individual support. A school counselor can also help in this area. Searching online for particular services can help, whether it is a specific type of crisis hotline or other mental health service.

Seeking support from friends, family, or teachers can be very helpful for people going through the healing process, but there are other resources that reach beyond familiar circles.

SEEKING HEALTH PROFESSIONALS

Some people may feel uncomfortable talking to strangers, regardless of whether or not it is an anonymous setting. But the people closest to a victim aren't necessary equipped to help. A good place to start is at school.

Some schools have help hotlines, guidance counselors, or psychiatrists who can meet with students to facilitate the healing process. If they also aren't well-

If you are concerned about staying anonymous, seeking advice from a telephone helpline can be a good way to seek help.

equipped for the issue, they can at least help with seeking help elsewhere by guiding the victim through searching the internet or finding other local counselors or mental health professionals.

Doctors and counselors can also provide various forms of therapy, offer recommendations for other health services, and in some cases, offer their patients medicine. Some doctors are trained to help people deal with emotional issues that result from all kinds of cyber-bullying.

Visiting one of these professionals regularly may offer relief until a victim feels the issues are resolved.

The type of help a victim of trolls and cyber-mobs should seek from an organization, other than a doctor, depends on the victimization he or she faced. For example, people in the LGBTQ community may benefit more from support groups for their community. A few national organizations that offer crisis intervention, suicide prevention, and aware-ness programs for LGBTQ youth include the Trevor

Dan Savage is the founder of the It Gets Better Project, dedicated to offering support to youth in the LGBTQ community.

Project and the It Gets Better Project. Similarly, support groups exist for encouraging a positive body image, as well as for other commonly targeted aspects of a person's identity.

COPING WITH FEELINGS

According to *Psychology Today* magazine, emotional distress can come across in many ways. This includes anger, sadness, anxiety, and even addictions and self-harming behaviors. A professional can help guide you through these difficult feelings and coping mechanisms, making sure that you are safe and deal with any self-harm or addictions that may occur. This means being aware of how badly the cyber trolling impacts the victim and understanding the urgency of the need to seek different forms of help.

Experts in psychology say that it can take up to 15 sessions—definitely more than one—of seeing a professional and discussing a problem to see that translate into change in a person's life. Most therapy simply involves talking about your feelings in a group or individually with a therapist. Some therapies are covered under insurance plans, but if cost is an issue, group therapies are usually less expensive than private sessions. Keep with your therapy to see how being a victim of trolling or cybermobs really affected your life. Talking about the initial experience may be helpful, but there may be a rush of emotions that suddenly hits you weeks, months, or even many years later. This rush may happen on multiple occasions, and you may feel like you are reliving the experience each time. Each reminder of the experience may be a reminder of the feelings that went with that experience. Remember that healing takes time and that you must cope with the feelings as they come.

General stress relief can also be a useful way to help you heal from the problems you experienced. Exercising is one form of stress relief. Taking on new hobbies is another good way to get your mind off difficult memories. For some people, talking to people who have gone through the same things can relieve stress and make them feel less alone. Spending time being with friends and just having fun is also a good way to relieve stress.

HEALING A REPUTATION

When trolls and cybermobs engage in activities that ruin a person's reputation, it can be difficult to spring back from. It's nearly impossible to erase evidence of bad reviews or slanderous comments from the internet. The difficulty of entering a relationship in the future or of finding a job lasts a long time. Revenge porn is difficult to remove, for example, and you cannot easily change the hurtful posts or images that come up when someone searches your name.

After alerting the authorities, a victim can take steps to recover from a problem like identity theft. Support

BECOMING AN EXAMPLE FOR OTHERS

In the late 1990s, White House intern Monica Lewinsky was thrust into the media headlines for what she admitted to be an inappropriate relationship with then president Bill Clinton. The scandal became known around the world and Lewinsky was sharply criticized for her ac-

After having been publicly shamed online, Monica Lewinsky stood up for the rights of cyber attack victims and became an antibullying advocate.

tions, and was subjected harsh cyberbullying. In an article in *Newsweek*, Lewinsky said of the experience, "I felt like every layer of my skin and my identity were ripped off of me in '98 and '99...It's a skinning of sorts. You feel incredibly raw and frightened. But I also feel like the shame sticks to you like tar." The experience made Lewinsky realize, years later, that she could use her notoriety and celebrity status to help victims of cyberbullying. She gave a TED Talk in 2015 about her experiences and the price of the shame she experienced through cyberbullying. Her efforts to help others who are cyberbullied or trolled continues to pay off. Lewinsky came out with a mobile phone app with special antibullying emojis, helping to raise awareness of how widespread and damaging the problem can be. Her efforts to be a positive role model help others who are in similar situations.

groups exist for people who have experienced identity theft. Making people aware of your identity theft problem is an important way to straighten out any problems it may have caused, like the impact of a poor credit score on the ability to get a loan.

The damage trolls and cybermobs do can be particularly damaging if you used your real name on social media sites because they are then attacking a real identity. At this point, it's not helpful to change your online identity to protect your real name, but getting positive posts and input from friends can bury the older posts beneath the new ones. The farther down the harassing posts or ones that misrepresent you are, the less likely someone will come across them when they search for your name. You can also try deleting the remaining posts that are damaging or blocking the people who put them up.

THE FUTURE OF TROLLING AND CYBERMOBS

Because trolling and cybermobs have become such a large problem, many computer companies are working to try to alleviate the problem and get rid of trolls before they can do too much damage. This would mean trying to identify and eliminate the trolls as soon as possible. A study from Stanford and Cornell Universities collected data after analyzing the comments sections of three websites. Two of the sites, Breitbart and CNN, are general news sites with reputations that precede them. The third site, IGN, is a news site focused on gaming. They analyzed nearly 39 million posts from 1.7 million users.

The study found that trolls had several features in common that could help the sites identify them in the future. Many seemed to have low readability scores with fewer positive words than other posts. They used more profanity and received more replies than other commenters. That's because their comments were deliberately inflammatory and damaging to others. Using these criteria can help computer programmers to create calculations or other problem-solving operations, called algorithms, to help them identify these particular

RitzyChunks: Cool video of space
April 14th, 2:30 PM

CoolBlaze: If you need some comic r
laughing out loud. My friend sent it to
work though. Proceed carefully! LOL h
April 15th, 1:05 AM

MajicElixr: Party safe tonight. As a than
I've put together a list of songs you can li
April 15th, 3:29 PM

Bordova: A little bit of social media can do
and see a very sweet video with some inter
April 16th, 11:00 AM

Ramsesthegreat: If this is web 2.0 then web
I hear everything will be in the cloud and it's n
Sounds like it's going to be really cool! 8) 64jh
April 16th, 4:11 PM

Kilik: Great list of the best and worst branding i
absolutely be there but there are others that are
63s2f4se
April 16th

Comment sections are a common playground for trolls. Trolls frequent them so much that patterns can categorize the types of messages that trolls leave and how they leave them.

users. This could be a way to find and ban the users before they do too much damage.

As of now, many web companies are reluctant to use algorithms to identify people who might exhibit characteristics of a troll. Many don't want to alienate their users before there is any evidence of wrongdoing or criminal activity. However, the possibility of focusing in on a certain type of user and his or her behavior is a possibility.

As long as the internet keeps making it possible for us to reach out to strangers and connect with people in a personal way, there will likely be bullies, trolls, and even cybermobs. While the internet can bring out the best in people, it can also bring out the worst. That's why it is important to be aware of the problem, do what we can to avoid it, and then recover from any damage to the best of our abilities. Helping other people get over their problems with trolls and cybermobs can also be the best way to get back at trolls and show that their behavior will not be accepted and that we can over-come the damaging effects of cyber harassment.

Cyber Rights Initiative A nonprofit organization dedicated to fighting online abuses and cyberbullying.

cyberbully A person who bullies someone online.

cybercrime unit A division of law enforcement that investigates cyber attacks and the work of criminals online.

cybermob A group of two or more people joining to harass or humiliate someone on the internet.

doxxing The practice of publishing someone's personal data online in an attempt to harass or humiliate.

Federal Bureau of Investigation (FBI) The federal law enforcement agency of the United States.

felony A crime that is more serious than a misdemeanor and may be punishable by jail time of a year or more.

flash mob A large public gathering that is organized online and suddenly carried out in person.

footprint The record of an event.

hacking In colloquial terms, gaining access to a computer system in order to steal or damage information; less colloquially, the act of writing code.

harassment Repeated, unwanted attention or pressure.

identity theft The illegal acquisition of someone's personal information for the purpose of posing as that person for personal and/or financial gain.

Intimate Privacy Protection Act A bill that has the potential to make it a crime to distribute pornography without the consent of the parties involved.

LGBTQ The acronym for lesbian, gay, bisexual, trans, and queer, a community of gender and sexual identities that share social or political concerns.

misdemeanor A minor legal offense that is punishable by up to a year in jail.

revenge porn Sexually explicit photos or video that someone shares online in an attempt to humiliate his or her former companion.

sexting The practice of sending someone sexually explicit photos or messages over a mobile device.

slander A false spoken statement that damages a person's reputation.

social media Websites, mobile device applications, and components of some video games that let users create and share content with each other.

swatting A form of harassment that involves calling emergency responders or SWAT teams to someone's home for false reasons.

troll A person who deliberately starts arguments or tries to upset people online with the intent of provoking one or many people or hurting their feelings.

Anti-Bullying Alliance
8 Wakley Street
London EC1V 7QE
England
Website: http://www.anti-bullyingalliance.org.uk/
This alliance is a coalition that fosters awareness of and
    training to combat bullying.

It Gets Better Project
110 S. Fairfax Avenue, Suite A11-71
Los Angeles, CA 90036
Website: http://www.itgetsbetter.org
This project is dedicated to supporting LGBTQ youth
    as they cope with harassment and other challenges
    that are common to being out.

National Crime Prevention Council
2614 Chapel Lake Drive, Suite B
Gambrills, MD 21054
(443) 292-4565
Website: http://www.ncpc.org
This organization is dedicated to keeping families
    and youth safe from crimes that involve violence,
    technology, theft, and other violations. It offers
    programs and trainings so that people are ready to
    deal with certain situations.

PrevNet
Queen's University
98 Barrie Street
Kingston, ON K7L 3N6
Canada
(613) 533-2632
Website: http://www.prevnet.ca
This is a Canadian network of research scientists and
 organizations that serve youth and are dedicated to
 stopping online bullying. They advocate for policy,
 and foster healthy relationships between peers.

Privacy and Access Council of Canada
Suite 330, Unit 440
10816 Macleod Trail
Calgary, AB T2J 5N8
Canada
(877) 746-7222
Website: https://pacc-ccap.ca
This is a nonprofit organization dedicated to privacy
 and access to information on the internet.

STOMP Out Bullying
220 East 57th Street, 9th Floor
Suite G
New York, NY 10022
(877) 602-8559
Website: http://www.stompoutbullying.org
STOMP Out Bullying is a leading national bullying and
 cyberbullying prevention organization for young
 people.

The Trevor Project
PO Box 69232
West Hollywood, CA 90069
(866) 488-7386
Website: www.thetrevorproject.org
This organization focuses on crisis intervention and
suicide prevention for teens and young adults. It
offers events and news updates to people who are
interested in latest developments in the LGBTQ
community.

WEBSITES

Because of the changing nature of internet links, Rosen
Publishing has developed an online list of websites
related to the subject of this book. This site is updated
regularly. Please use this link to access this list:

http://www.rosenlinks.com/NTKL/trolls

FOR FURTHER READING

Cohen Wood, Tyler. *Catching the Catfishers: Disarm the Online Pretenders, Predators, and Perpetrators Who Are Out to Ruin Your Life.* Wayne, NJ: Career Press, 2014.

Damour, Lisa. *Untangled: Guiding Teenage Girls Through the Seven Transitions into Adulthood.* New York: NY: Ballantine Books, 2016.

Hinduja, Sameer. *Bullying Beyond the Schoolyard: Preventing and Responding to Cyberbullying.* Newbury Park, CA: Corwin Publishing, 2014.

Hitchcock, J. A. *Cyberbullying and the Wild, Wild, Web: What Everyone Needs to Know.* Lanham, MD: Rowman & Littlefield Publishers, 2016.

Jacobs, Thomas A. *Teen Cyberbullying Investigated: Where Do Your Rights End and Consequences Begin?* Golden Valley, MN: Free Spirit Publishing, 2010.

Kowalski, Robin M. *Cyberbullying: Bullying in the Digital Age.* New York, NY: Wiley-Blackwell, 2012.

Patchin, Justin W. *Words Wound: Delete Cyberbullying and Make Kindness Go Viral.* Golden Valley, MN: Free Spirit Publishing, 2013.

Todd, Paula. *Extreme Mean: Trolls, Bullies, and Predators Online.* Oxford, UK: Signal Publishers, 2014.

Weckerle, Andrea. *Civility in the Digital Age: How Companies and People Can Triumph Over Haters, Trolls, Bullies, and Other Jerks.* London, UK: Que Publishing, 2013.

ABC News. "Bullying: Resources for How to Get Help."
    Retrieved October 1, 2016. http://abcnews.go.com
    /Entertainment/bullying-cyberbullying-resources
    /story?id=15962497.
About Psychotherapy. "How Long Does It Take?"
    Retrieved October 1, 2016. http://www
    .aboutpsychotherapy.com/Thowlong.php.
Bernstein, Elizabeth. "Why We Are So Rude Online."
    Wall Street Journal, October 2, 2012. http://www.wsj
    .com/articles/SB10000872396390444592404578030
    351784405148.
Bullying Statistics. "Cyber Bullying Statistics." Retrieved
    September 20, 2016. http://www.bullyingstatistics
    .org/content/cyber-bullying-statistics.html.
Citron, Danielle Keats. "How Cyber Mobs and Trolls
    Have Ruined the Internet—and Destroyed Lives."
    Newsweek, September 19, 2014. http://www
    .newsweek.com/internet-and-golden-age
    -bully-271800.
Cyber Civil Rights Initiative. "34 States + DC Have
    Revenge Porn Laws." Retrieved October 1, 2016.
    https://www.cybercivilrights.org/revenge-porn-laws.
Fairbairn, Emily. "Revenge Porn Suicide Shame." *The Sun*,
    September 16, 2016. https://www.thesun.co.uk/living
    /1799725/tiziana-cantone-killed-herself-over-leaked
    -sex-tape-because-in-italy-sex-for-fun-is-still-a-sin/.
Fight the New Drug. "Press Send: Real Stories of Sex-
    ting & Revenge Porn." January 16, 2015. http://
    fightthenewdrug.org/sexting-and-revenge-porn/.

FindLaw. "Cyberbullying." Retrieved September 20, 2016. http://criminal.findlaw.com/criminal-charges /cyber-bullying.html.

Firger, Jessica. "Monica Lewinsky Speaks Out Against Cyberbullying in a Revealing Interview." *Newsweek*, April 16, 2016. http://www.newsweek.com /monica-lewinsky-speaks-out-against-cyberbullying -revealing-interview-448655.

Followill, Peter. "Harassment and Cyberbullying as Crimes." *Criminal Defense Lawyer*, Retrieved October 5, 2016. http://www.criminaldefenselawyer.com /crime-penalties/federal/harassment.htm#.

Grimminck, Robert. "10 Notorious Internet Trolls Who Were Exposed." *Listverse*, August 8, 2015. http://list verse.com/2015/08/08/10-notorious-internet-trolls -who-were-exposed/.

Isaac, Mike. "Twitter Bars Milo Yiannopoulos in Wake of Leslie Jones's Report of Abuse." *New York Times*, July 20, 2016. http://www.nytimes .com/2016/07/20/technology/twitter-bars -milo-yiannopoulos-in-crackdown-on-abusive -comments.html?_r=0.

It Gets Better. "What Is the It Gets Better Project?" Retrieved October 1, 2016. http://www.itgetsbetter .org/pages/about-it-gets-better-project/.

Morrison, Kimberlee. "Could Algorithms Be the Future of Troll Catching?" *Ad Week*, April 22, 2015. http:// www.adweek.com/socialtimes/could-algorithms-be -the-future-of-troll-catching/619193.

National Crime Prevention Council. "What Parents Can Do About Cyberbullying." Retrieved October 1,

2016. http://www.ncpc.org/topics/cyberbullying
/stop-cyberbullying.

Smith, Gerry. "Now Women Are Getting Arrested for
Revenge Porn." *Huffington Post*, October 21, 2014.
http://www.huffingtonpost.com/2014/10/21/revenge
-porn-arrests_n_6016946.html.

Snider, Brett. "Can You Sue Anonymous Internet Trolls?"
FindLaw, October 30, 2014. http://blogs.findlaw
.com/law_and_life/2014/10/can-you-sue
-anonymous-internet-trolls.html.

Wanshel, Elyse. "Teen Makes 'Sit With Us' App That
Helps Lunch Buddies." *Huffington Post*, September
27, 2016. http://www.huffingtonpost.com/entry/teen
-creates-app-sit-with-us-open-welcoming-tables
-lunch-bullying_us_57c5802ee4b09cd22d926463.

Wilson, Mark. "Are You an Internet 'Troll'? Legal Consequences to Consider." *FindLaw*, October 21, 2014.
http://blogs.findlaw.com/law_and_life/2014/10
/are-you-an-internet-troll-legal-consequences-to
-consider.html.

ABOUT THE AUTHOR

Sabrina Adams has written books for teens on how to break into sports law, be awarded with internship offers, and choose a vocational technology track for success in business. She graduated from Fordham University and lives in upstate New York with her husband and two sons.

PHOTO CREDITS